What If?

310 Bite-Size Brain Snacks To Spark Your Creative Spirit

Written & Designed by
Susan Le Page Simmons

Illustrated by
Jeremy Le Page

I.C. Creative!
The Simmons Group

What If? 310 Bite-Size Brain Snacks To Spark Your Creative Spirit
Copyright © 1994 by Susan Le Page Simmons.
Illustrations by Jeremy Le Page and used by permission.
All rights reserved.

First Printing: June, 1994
Published in Canada by
I.C. Creative! The Simmons Group

Canadian Cataloguing in Publication Data
Simmons, Susan Le Page, 1954—
What If? 310 Bite-Size Brain Snacks To Spark Your Creative Spirit
ISBN 0-9698446-0-3
1. Creative ability. 2. Creative thinking.
I. Le Page, Jeremy, 1974—
II. Title.
BF408.S55 1995   153.3'5   C94-931482-X

Remarks from some of the world's great creative thinkers:

"As someone who has asked for years, 'What would happen if our knees bent the other way?', Susan's bite-size brain snacks are nutritious enough to serve as a main course. Bon appetit!"—MICHAEL MCKINLEY, CSP, CPAE, President, McKinley Companies, Inc.

"A delightful, whimsical collection of thought-provoking ideas to ponder. 'What If' is pure creativity."—ELIZABETH JEFFRIES, CSP, Author of THE HEART OF LEADERSHIP

"What if you read and use this book? You'll learn, laugh and be much better for the experience."—W.E. (BILL) HARMER, Speaker, The Harmer Group

"Being more creative and having more fun are two things we all need to do more often. This book will help you with both."—RICK BARRERA, CSP

"A wonderful book! Thanks for helping me see the world again as I did as a child."—MAURICE O'CALLAGHAN, Speaker

"What if...you read this...and it helped?!"—JACK DONOHUE, Coach

"Thoughts to grow by, or thoughts to refresh and refocus."—TOM STOYAN, Author of SELL MORE, 101 IDEAS TO INCREASE SALES NOW!

"Reading Susan's book makes me feel good all over."—PETER URS BENDER, Author of SECRETS OF POWER PRESENTATIONS

"A daily dosage of Susan's mind openers is exactly what we need."—BILL GIBSON, Author of BOOST YOUR BUSINESS IN ANY ECONOMY and HOW TO GET A JOB IN ANY ECONOMY

"Loaded with fun, packed with spirit, rich with inspiration...qualities this book shares with its author."—ALAN SIMMONS, CSP, Speaker/husband/ pretty insightful guy

"What if I just sit here until someone notices me?"—DINO SIMMONS, #1 Cat

Acknowledgments

I am grateful to a bunch of people whose support, encouragement and enthusiasm helped to get this little book into your hands. They include:

Joe McCulloch and your team at The Vincent Press Ltd.—thanks for giving this CFH extraordinary customer service and attention.

Gregory J.P. Godek (bestselling author of 1001 Ways To Be Romantic)—thank you for your unbelievable generosity of spirit and guidance.

Karen, Marilyn, Lorna, Erin, Lina, Alan, Andrew, Jeremy—some of you were proofers, some of you encouragers; most of you were a steady source of both. Thanks to those who knew when to give what...and did.

Rosita, Mike, Lance, Mitchell, Harold, Jim, Scott, Dave, Elizabeth, Rick, Jack, Tom, Bill, Maurice, Peter, Bill—I appreciate each one of you.

Vickie Coulson at Coles The Book People—thank you.

Dan Bristow—your amazing 'no problem' attitude means more than you'll ever know. Thanks for the countless hours of effort, and for making me laugh when we thought I'd drive both of us crazy.

Alan, Jeremy, Dan, Dan and Andrew *("What if I walked this way all the time?")*—my heartfelt appreciation for your laughter, creative input, tolerance, and willingness to jump in and help with just about anything.

And to our young friend, Dan Driscoll—this one's for you.

For my A.P.P. Jack—
Always the love,
Always the laughter.
LYG,
Syd

Warm-up exercises:

❑ What if you decide to change some of your old habits, old ways of doing things, old ways of thinking?

❑ What if you do use this book as a tool for:
  ✓ Laughter?
  ✓ Positive change?
  ✓ Personal growth?
  ✓ Finding new ways to approach your challenges?
  ✓ Sparking that wonderful, unlimited creative spirit?

❑ What if you begin each morning with "What if...?"

Introduction

WHAT IF the way to solve a problem was to turn it inside out? What if we talked with each other more often, listened to each other more carefully, and together explored the power of imagination? What if whimsical thinking could take you to unexpected places of accomplishment? Sounds easy—if it weren't so silly.

Sometimes we get so caught up in doing the right thing, the best thing, the wisest or the safest thing that we overlook the obvious and bury the absurd under heaps of—well—adultness. We forget to shake off the layers and dig for that rare and limitless nugget of truth. It's called simplicity. It's called hmmmm. And therein lies the magic of *possibility*.

Our hope is you'll discover a couple of gems in this book and use them to spark the creative spirit in your corner of the world. If all you find is a laugh or two, that's okay. This is a time when we can all use a little extra laughter.

Oh, and do us a favour, will you? Share this book with someone who's in search of his or her own possibilities. Because when all is said and written, the gift of encouragement is the greatest what-if of all.

—Susan

What if ...

1. Your bones were on the outside?

2. Jelly beans were nutritious?

3. You never ever blamed anything on anybody else?

"You and I have a choice.
Either we lament all the high notes we can't or won't hit,
or we leave those to Pavarotti
and get on with the rest of our song."

Rosita Perez, CPAE

What if...

4. The United Nations called to ask your advice?

5. Everyone's first name was Bob?

6. You always remembered to say, "Thank you"?

What if, at eight o'clock tomorrow morning, I...

_____

_____

_____

What if...

7. Your eyes crossed every time you complained?

8. You were unable to speak for an entire day?

9. Broccoli tasted like chocolate?

What if I spent less time...

_____

_____

and more time...

_____

_____

What if...

10. You had to wear shoes on your hands?

11. You kept a penguin as a house pet?

12. Before today is over, you tell someone,
    "I appreciate you"?

"Nothing great was ever achieved without enthusiasm."

Ralph Waldo Emmerson

What if...

13. For the next five days, you count the number of times that you begin a sentence with "My" or "I"?

14. You gave the absolute best of yourself to every relationship?

15. You smiled every time you passed someone in the grocery store aisles?

What if, tomorrow, I didn't wear any...

_____

_____

_____

What if ...

16. You looked at the situation from the other guy's point of view?

17. Coffee and doughnut shop employees were always friendly to their customers?

18. Your behavior showed that you never take anyone for granted?

What if ...

19. Cars and trucks were made out of bouncy rubber material?

20. Dandelions grew as big as trees?

21. Your cat could tell you a story about his/her day?

What if I used a creative approach to my relationship with...

_____

_____

_____

What if ...

22. The Queen of England called to say she was coming over for a slumber party?

23. You weren't afraid of the bogeyman?

24. You wore your pyjamas to work?

"Behold, I do not give lectures or a little charity,
When I give, I give myself."

Walt Whitman

What if ...

25. You wrote a love note to your favourite pal every morning?

26. You automatically treated everyone with courtesy and respect?

27. You actually do stay in touch with people when you say you will?

What if I make a spontaneous visit to...

_____

_____

_____

What if ...

28. You kept every promise you ever made?

29. You applauded someone else's annoying habits?

30. You counted your blessings before you got out of bed in the morning?

What if I did something to nurture my love of...

_____

_____

_____

What if...

31. Before you said something negative,
    you phrased it in a positive way?

32. Snoring sounded like laughter?

33. You saved every coin you ever found?

"My name is Might-have-been;
I am also called No-more, Too-late, Farewell."

Dante Gabriel Rossetti

What if...

34. You had to eat egg rolls and lobster and pistachio pudding for breakfast?

35. You did have bells on your toes?

36. You could change your biggest regret?

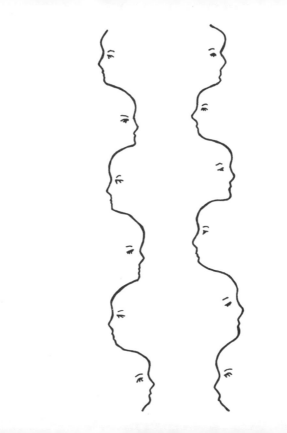

What if ...

37. You had the use of your neighbour's credit card for a day?

38. You discovered a way to cure rudeness?

39. It snowed marshmallows on New Year's Day?

What if, just for laughs, I...

_____

_____

_____

What if ...

    40.   Problems made sounds?

    41.   You had five eyes?

    42.   You could choose your parents and siblings?

What if I used ten dollars to help...

_____

_____

_____

What if...

43. Twelve guys named Bubba showed up
    singing "Happy Birthday"...and it wasn't
    your birthday?

44. You found a salamander in your salad?

45. Rainbows only came in one colour?

"The myth of the impossible dream
is more powerful than all the facts of history. "
Robert Fulghum

What if...

46. There were no rules?

47. Purple steam shot out your nose whenever you got angry?

48. Orange steam shot out your nose whenever you felt jealous?

What if I changed these old habits...

_____

_____

_____

What if...

49. You made your own good luck?

50. Everyone in the world took responsibility for their words and actions?

51. It rained only at night?

What if I invited...

_____

_____

_____

What if...

52. You had an Attitude Adjustment Button that other people could push?

53. There were no numbers?

54. You began doing *the opposite?*

What if...

55. Birds buzzed, bees sang and bugs whistled "Dixie"?

56. Paper were alive?

57. You could choose one day to live over?

"It is only with the heart that one can see rightly;
what is essential is invisible to the eye."

The Little Prince

What if...

58. You never took your frustrations, fears or anger out on anyone else?

59. You could be recycled?

60. Everyone took turns being the boss?

What if I used laughter to:

_____

_____

_____

What if ...

61. You could trade places with your dog for a day?

62. You made one anonymous and kind gesture towards a different person every day?

63. You find out who "they" are?

What if I changed the way I...

_____

_____

_____

What if ...

64. Somebody named a ship after you?

65. There were no colours?

66. You opened the Sunday comics and found a caricature of yourself?

"Today I will try really hard to remember
that the tail that looks so tempting is my own,
and I have already caught it."

Michael Cader

What if ...

67. You replaced the word *hate* with the word *pickle?*

68. You knew the lyrics to every song ever written?

69. You woke up in the night and discovered you had eaten your pillow?

What if I imagined a new way of...

_____

_____

_____

What if ...

70. You became invisible and overheard a conversation about you?

71. Everyone had enough to eat?

72. You approached each problem with: "What can I do to make this better"?

What if ...

73. Your actions spoke of patience, caring
and understanding?

74. You woke up in a different country and
didn't know where you were?

75. You never complain about how sick, busy,
tired, fat, thin, frustrated, overworked,
underpaid, bored, green or purple you are?

What if I opened my mind more about...

_____

_____

_____

What if ...

76. You take what you've learned from your mistakes and use it to create a better "next time"?

77. It was safe to go anywhere, anytime?

78. You could grant your best friend a wish?

"It's not what happens to you.
It's what you do about it."

W Mitchell

What if ...

79. You could trust everyone?

80. There were only twenty days in each month?

81. Your refrigerator spoke to you when you opened the door?

What if I made a greater effort to...

_____

_____

_____

What if...

82.   You could store courage in a peanut butter jar?

83.   Clocks worked backwards?

84.   You were a worm?

What if I gave more credit to...

_____

_____

_____

What if...

85. You could take photographs with your eyes?

86. You could buy self-esteem at the drug store?

87. Your elbows and knees bent the other way?

"Experience is the child of Thought,
and Thought is the child of Action."

Benjamin Disraeli

What if ...

88. Your great, great-grandmother wrote a letter to you?

89. You made ten people laugh every day?

90. All fattening foods smelled like skunks?

What if ...

91. Fingernails grew across your forehead?

92. Burps exterminated termites?

93. Everybody in the world stood on their heads at precisely the same moment?

What if I listened more carefully to...

_____

_____

_____

What if...

94. Rocks resembled human beings...or vice versa?

95. The passenger seated next to you on a plane was a monkey?

96. You found out that your physician moonlighted as a stand-up comedian?

What if I paid more attention to...

_____

_____

_____

What if ...

97. You could speak twelve languages?

98. You had big feathery wings?

99. There were no shopping malls?

What if I wrote a letter to...

_____

_____

_____

What if ...

    100. Money evaporated if you didn't spend it within a week?

    101. Your ears fell off when you didn't listen to somebody who was talking to you?

    102. You could help to make a miracle happen?

What if I sent a coupon for one...

_____

to...

_____

What if ...

103. We grew wheels instead of feet?

104. At the age of 30, we possessed the wisdom of a 60 year old?

105. At the age of 40, we had to re-enter kindergarten?

What if I called...

_____

and said....

_____

_____

_____

What if ...

106. You teach the people in your life
to take responsibility for themselves?

107. You could walk anywhere in the world in
half an hour?

108. Your bellybutton were magnetic?

What if ...

109. Out of every pay cheque, you give ten dollars to someone who needs it more than you do?

110. We lived on the bottom of the ocean?

111. You were permitted to have only one *feel sorry for yourself* day per decade?

"When Imagination walks, she writes letters to the earth.
When she runs, her feet trace postcards to the sun."

J. Ruth Gendler

What if ...

112. You had just one chance to tell your friend
something you've never told him or her?

113. The phone book rhymed?

114. Toothpaste looked like tar and tasted
like asparagus?

What if I sent...

_____

_____

_____

What if...

115. Hair felt like candyfloss?

116. Goldfish told jokes?

117. Finger foods were?

What if I kick up my heels and...

_____

_____

_____

What if...

118. *Cat* was spelled d-o-g?

119. Envelopes tasted good when you licked them?

120. We crawled on our arms?

"The vitality of thought is in adventure.
Ideas won't keep. Something must be done about them. "
Alfred North Whitehead

What if ...

121. The sky was green, the grass was blue and trees looked like peacocks?

122. Food in restaurants looked like the pictures on the menu?

123. You heard a choir sing each time you forgave someone?

What if I pretended I was a...

_____

_____

_____

What if ...

124. You had to wear a Hoola-hoop® around your neck every time you expressed a nasty thought?

125. Politicians' voices went up three octaves when they didn't tell the truth?

126. The mute button on the television remote worked on people?

What if ...

127. Every second month was July?

128. The Easter Bunny showed up at your dinner table?

129. They threw a surprise party for you and forgot
to invite you?

What if I take absolute responsibility for...

_____

_____

_____

What if ...

130. Dust bunnies came to life during the night?

131. Kangaroos were letter carriers?

132. You really did save for a rainy day?

What if I forget my fears and...

_____

_____

_____

What if...

133. People said, "Why didn't I think of that?"
     about something you actually did?

134. Everybody took the same two weeks for vacation?

135. There was a food fight in your refrigerator
     after you went to bed?

What if I put more faith in...

_____

_____

_____

What if...

136. Trees do make a noise when they fall in the forest and no one is there to hear?

137. Your life depended on you having a clear conscience?

138. Cheese could sing?

What if I surprised...

_____

_____

_____

What if ...

139. Potatoes could see with their eyes?

140. People told you what they really thought about you?

141. Ideas came in bubbles?

"To be what we are,
and to become what we are capable of becoming,
is the only end of life."

Robert Louis Stevenson

What if ...

142. Appreciation could be gift-wrapped?

143. An alarm went off if you didn't wash your hands in public restrooms?

144. You sent a thank you note to everyone who ever taught you something?

What if ...

145. You did get your nose stuck in
     someone else's business?

146. Ice cubes were hot?

147. Your feet did go to sleep?

What if I followed my heart and...

_____

_____

_____

What if ...

148. You did get pins and needles in your hands?

149. True love always was?

150. You had to learn to walk and talk all over again?

What if I said I was sorry to...

_____

_____

_____

What if...

151. People did behave exactly the way you think
     they should?

152. Cobwebs were made of spun silver?

153. You could hear through an ear of corn?

"The true value in ideas rests not in their existence—
but in your willingness to use them."

Alan Simmons, CSP

What if...

154. Ice cream tasted like mustard?

155. You had to make up for any unkind word
you'd ever spoken?

156. It were true every time someone said,
"I'm only trying to help..."?

What if I said, "I love you" to...

_____

_____

_____

What if ...

157. You never got any second chances?

158. With a snap of your fingers, you could shrink to the size of a walnut or grow to the size of a barn?

159. You gave yourself an entire play day to do anything you wanted?

What if...

160. You had to teach someone a new hobby?

161. Other peoples' children were as delightful
as their parents thought they were?

162. Your partner always left love notes under
your pillow when he/she went on a trip?

What if I spent tomorrow...

_____

_____

_____

What if ...

163. You always send love notes for your partner
to open when he/she is on a trip?

164. The person next to you could hear your thoughts?

165. Your political leader turned into a tuna whenever
election promises weren't carried through?

"It's not easy being green."

Kermit The Frog

What if ...

166. Your loyalty and honesty could be measured with a thermometer?

167. You always behaved as if the whole world was watching you?

168. You finished every project, book or diet you ever began?

What if I told...

_____

that I appreciate...

_____

What if ...

169. You were the Wizard of Oz?

170. You had no place to sleep tonight?

171. The only life you tried to control was your own?

What if I forgave...

_____

_____

_____

What if...

172. Your tongue swelled up when you criticized
somebody?

173. Gravity stopped one day per month but you
never knew when it would happen?

174. You never said, "If only..." or "Someday when..."?

What if...

175. Turtles drove taxis?

176. There was such a thing as an integrity implant?

177. You could drive a flying saucer from midnight
to six o'clock in the morning?

"Life is not orderly.
No matter how we try to make life so,
right in the middle of it we die, lose a leg, fall in love,
drop a jar of applesauce..."

Natalie Goldberg

What if ...

178. You woke up as a rooster?

179. You really could hitch your wagon to a star?

180. You could spend an entire afternoon with Albert Einstein?

What if I talked with my family about...

_____

_____

_____

What if...

181. You dialed into voice mail and couldn't get out?

182. You really could escape when you hit that key on your computer?

183. Instead of complaining about someone, you paid that person a compliment?

What if it were possible for me to...

_____

_____

_____

What if ...

184. You did treat people the way you wanted
them to treat you?

185. AIDS could be cured by the power of prayer?

186. You were known as a person who inspires peace?

"Imagination
is more important than knowledge."

Albert Einstein

What if ...

187. Leopards could change their spots?

188. Your bathroom mirror reflected your character?

189. You asked somebody how they were,
     and you cared about the reply?

What if...

190. You were somebody's pet peeve?

191. You realize how much of you there is to give to the world?

192. The sun shone whenever you put on your sunglasses?

What if I threw out my...

_____

_____

_____

What if ...

193. You did think of others before yourself?

194. You did your share to prevent *political correctness* from replacing common sense?

195. Love was stronger than death?

What if I stopped being so darn careful about...

_____

_____

_____

What if ...

196. You received a fax response to a prayer?

197. You received a fax response to a prayer,
but you didn't have a fax machine?

198. Nobody ever told you what to do—
and you never told anybody else what to do?

"Change everything,
except your loves."

Voltaire

What if...

    199. You followed your heart's desire?

    200. You could toboggan on a cloud?

    201. You had to give a speech on zymology?

What if I took a chance and...

_____

_____

_____

What if ...

202. Mosquitos drank mint julep?

203. Everybody had pink hair?

204. Leprechauns rode unicorns?

What if ...

205. Wheels were oblong?

206. You lost your freedom?

207. You were only allowed to worry on an
      Official Worry Day?

What if I risked disapproval and...

_____

_____

_____

What if ...

208. You became a national authority on pelicans?

209. You could be or do anything in the whole wide world?

210. Zebras were really horses in jail?

"Two roads diverged in a wood, and I,
I took the one less travelled by,
and that has made all the difference."

Robert Frost

What if ...

211. Therewasnopunctuationorspacesbetweenwords

212. You took a mud bath and got stuck up to your shoulders?

213. The ghosts of Christmas Past, Present and Future paid you a visit on December 24?

What if I gave myself permission to...

_____

_____

_____

What if ...

214. You could trust everyone to always tell you the truth?

215. You could take a tour through time?

216. The moon told you a secret?

What if I gave a little more...

_____

_____

_____

What if ...

217. You could buy a Thinking Cap?

218. You replaced the word *but* with the word *and?*

219. You removed the words *can't* and *I can't help it* from your vocabulary?

What if...

220. Scissors stayed sharp?

221. Other people work as hard as you think you do?

222. Tape didn't stick?

"If life had a second edition,
how I would correct the proofs."

John Clare

What if...

223. Socks came out of the dryer in pairs?

224. There were no countries and no borders?

225. You found a way to save one child from neglect or abuse?

What if I took a big red crayon and...

_____

_____

_____

What if...

226. The world was free of conflict for a day?

227. You made only positive choices?

228. Nobody ever picked you first?

What if I let go of...

_____

_____

_____

What if...

229. You could draw a map of the human soul?

230. Even in little ways, you were never a nay-sayer, discourager or critic?

231. You could exercise in your sleep?

"Curiosity is one of the permanent and certain characteristics of a vigorous mind."

Samuel Johnson

What if ...

232. You could be somebody else for a day?

233. A single gesture of your generosity helped to change the course of someone else's life?

234. Everybody quit?

What if...

235. You always chose on the side of fairness?

236. You never whined or grumbled out loud?

237. You look for something good in every
person you meet?

What if I bought a big bouquet of flowers and...

_____

_____

_____

What if ...

238. People never forgave you for your mistakes?

239. You did turn your problems inside-out?

240. You were a private detective for a day?

What if I closed my eyes and remembered the time...

_____

_____

_____

What if ...

241. Your words and actions showed genuine interest in the other person's life?

242. You did something to help someone else's career?

243. Crocodiles could tap dance?

"Great spirits have always encountered
violent opposition from mediocre minds."

Albert Einstein

What if ...

244. Real heroes are people we never hear about?

245. You always took the extra time to read the instructions?

246. The earth was shaped like a football?

What if I bought a book about...

_____

and gave it to...

_____

What if ...

247. You never had a bad idea?

248. Every day you tell somebody how wonderful, thoughtful or valuable you think they are?

249. You always acted upon your instincts?

What if...

250. Flatulence was colourful?

251. It rained so much that you had to build an ark?

252. You do become someone's guardian angel
after you die?

What if I bought a big can of paint and...

_____

_____

_____

What if ...

253. You had to pay a fine any time you made an incorrect assumption?

254. Dawn cracked, night fell and midnight stroked?

255. We had to read upside down?

"Some night soon, look to a star—
In it, you will find laughter again.
For this, after all,
Is the reason I was here."

Susan Simmons

What if ...

256. It was so windy that your hat blew all the way to Mississippi?

257. You got whirling around in a revolving door and you couldn't get out?

258. You turned into a frog when someone kissed you?

What if I curled up in my favourite chair and...

_____

_____

_____

What if ...

259. You could move mountains?

260. Retail, government and public service employees were paid according to the level of customer service they provide?

261. You woke up in a jungle where a cigar-smoking tiger asked you what time it was?

What if I got three friends together and...

_____

_____

_____

What if...

262. A *60 Minutes* camera crew actually did
     show up at your front door?

263. There were no such thing as credit cards?

264. You packed all your troubles in an old kit bag?

What if ...

265. There were no government hand-outs?

266. Health care professionals only had to
      concentrate on taking care of their patients?

267. Life were a figment of your imagination?

What if I picked up the phone and...

_____

_____

_____

What if ...

268. Government leaders solved problems?

269. You do something to help someone who's vision impaired?

270. Before today is over, you say, "I love you" to the most important people in your life?

"Without this playing with fantasy,
no creative work has ever yet come to birth.
The debt we owe to the play of imagination is incalculable."
Carl Gustav Jung

What if ...

271. You did use your talents and gifts to their full potential?

272. Judgment does say more about you than those you judge?

273. You valued people as if they were precious treasures?

What if I told...

_____

that I'd really like to...

_____

What if ...

274. You sent someone a little present for no reason?

275. People looked down on you just because of your race or religion?

276. You never said, "It's not my fault," "It's not my job," "It's not my problem," or "It's not my responsibility."?

What if I said, "Thank you" to...

_____

for...

_____

What if ...

277. You had to sacrifice a year of your life to achieve your biggest goal?

278. You took a public stand for something in which you believed?

279. Tomorrow morning, you do something new to cultivate your spirit of adventure?

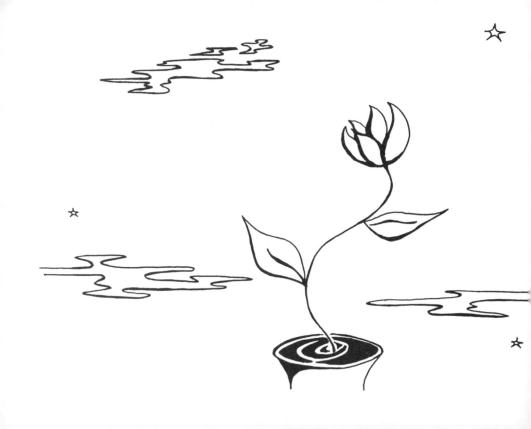

What if ...

280. You lost your sense of humour?

281. Everything you do tomorrow is fun,
silly or spontaneous?

282. You make a commitment to open your
mind a little wider each day?

What if I looked for the fun in...

_____

_____

_____

What if ...

283. Your smile could ease someone's pain—
but you never knew when, why or where?

284. By adjusting your priorities, you could
live *happily ever after*?

285. We could see fireflies in the daylight?

What if I bought two round-trip tickets to...

_____

_____

_____

What if ...

286. You took pride in everything you did?

287. You did have potatoes growing in your ears?

288. You behave as though you believe anything
is possible?

What if a kid I know what-iffed about...

_____

_____

_____

What if ...

289. You could forget your head if it weren't attached?

290. You left a legacy of unconditional love?

291. You made yourself known as an *I'll do it,
no problem* person?

"Thunder is good, thunder is impressive;
but it is lightning that does the work."

Mark Twain

What if ...

292. You could always count on your brother or sister to stick up for you?

293. The only way to see was through your heart?

294. You looked for the *best way* instead of *your way?*

What if ...

295. You took special care to never discount anyone else's feelings?

296. The best things in life weren't free?

297. Your most attractive quality is the way others feel when they're with you?

What if I expressed more...

_____

_____

_____

What if ...

298. You had to live without any electrical appliances?

299. Police uniforms included beehive hairstyles?

300. You strived to be the MVP at your place of work?

What if I were more thoughtful about the way I...

_____

_____

_____

What if...

301. You cried out for help and nobody responded?

302. A polar bear greeted you in your shower?

303. You look for what you *can* do, what you *do* have, and how *you can* make yourself a little happier?

What if...

_____

_____

_____

What if ...

304. Trains flew in the air and planes ran on tracks?

305. You always make sure that you're the first one to apologize?

306. Your mother did have eyes in the back of her head?

What if...

_____

_____

_____

What if ...

307. You watched a new television sitcom and discovered the story was based on your life?

308. You caught a fish and it screamed, "Ouch! My lip, my lip!"?

309. Your most endearing quality was your obvious love of life?

What if ...

310. Before today is over—
      You mend one fence that you left for broken,
      or rebuild one bridge that you helped to burn?

      Think about it.
      What if?

"As you live your life from this moment to the next,
Please think about those whose paths you cross.
Even if they stand right in front of you,
Take one little step that can,
And will,
Make all the difference in the world."

From: The Friendship Wish
by Susan Simmons

About the Illustrator & Author

Jeremy is one of those rare individuals who, simply by example, continues to teach us much about kindness, loyalty and sensitivity. He is the creator of the yet-to-be published, *Barley & Francis*, a funny and inspiring illustrated children's tale of acceptance and friendship.

Jeremy cooks a mean bowl of pasta and has recently begun to wear matching socks. His plans include college, along with the pursuit of his love of music, writing and art. He is the son of Susan Simmons and artist, Eddie Le Page, brother of artist, Erin, and friend/stepson of Alan and Kim.

Susan is the creator of the *Friendship Wish,* the *Keep In Touch* card collection, and *What If? Bite-Size Brain Snacks.* A founding member and former director of Idea Connection Ltd. Speakers Bureau, she now runs I.C. Creative!, the marketing division of The Simmons Group.

Susan is a mystery novel addict who dislikes cold Canadian winters but neither she, nor her Siamese cat, Dino, can get anyone to take them seriously about the weather thing. Her three greatest blessings and sources of inspiration are Erin, Jeremy and Alan.

Both Susan and Jeremy began their lives in Dundas, Ontario. They currently live in Peterborough, Ontario, Canada.

P.S.

1. **What If?** 310 Bite-Size Brain Snacks is available at quantity discount with bulk purchases for business, educational or promotional use.
2. We'll be happy to connect you with our illustrator should you be in need of his artistic talents.
3. A portion of **What If?** proceeds will be donated to a worthy cause.
4. More great products available from The Simmons Group:

—**The Keep In Touch Collection**—
Any Occasion Cards To Inspire The Heart & Mind
Written by Susan Simmons, illustrated by Erin Le Page.
—**There Are No Secrets**—
Universal Laws To Use Every Day
Action-oriented audio cassette learning system by Alan Simmons, CSP.

All products and presentations are backed by our famous 100% Guarantee.

The Simmons Group

P.O. Box 894 ● Peterborough ● Ontario ● Canada ● K9J 7A2
Customer Service Hotlines: 1-800-661-6767 ● 1-800-361-1203 (U.S. & Canada)
Fax (705) 743-1964